GHOST STORIES

GHOSTS IN CEMETERIES

By Lisa Owings

EPIC

BELLWETHER MEDIA • MINNEAPOLIS, MN

EPIC BOOKS are no ordinary books. They burst with intense action, high-speed heroics, and shadows of the unknown. Are you ready for an Epic adventure?

Library of Congress Cataloging-in-Publication Data

Names: Owings, Lisa, author.
Title: Ghosts in Cemeteries / by Lisa Owings.
Description: Minneapolis, MN : Bellwether Media, Inc., [2017] | Series: Epic.
  Ghost Stories | Includes bibliographical references and index. | Audience:
  Age: 7-12.
Identifiers: LCCN 2015045548 | ISBN 9781626174276 (hardcover : alk. paper)
Subjects: LCSH: Haunted cemeteries–United States–Juvenile literature. |
  Ghosts–United States–Juvenile literature.
Classification: LCC BF1474.3 .O95 2017 | DDC 133.1/22–dc23
LC record available at http://lccn.loc.gov/2015045548

Printed in the United States of America, North Mankato, MN.

TABLE OF CONTENTS

REST IN PEACE

You stroll past a cemetery at night. There is a flash of movement. You turn. But nothing is there. Was it a ghost?

Cemeteries are resting places for the dead. Do spirits wander among the graves?

VOODOO QUEEN

Marie Laveau lived in New Orleans in the 1800s. She was famous for practicing **voodoo**. She helped people by performing **rituals** and spells.

Marie Laveau

New Orleans, Louisiana

Laveau died in 1881. She is likely buried in St. Louis Cemetery No. 1.

St. Louis Cemetery No. 1

GOSSIP QUEEN

Laveau worked as a hairdresser. Some say she used customers' gossip to appear all-knowing.

HISTORY CONNECTION

Voodoo beliefs came to New Orleans from Africa and Haiti. The religion involves charms thought to heal or protect from harm.

ST. JOHN'S EVE

Each June 23, Laveau performed special rituals. Her ghost may still lead followers in worship on this day.

Some believe Laveau's ghost haunts her grave. They recognize her by the **tignon** she wears. They say Laveau still helps those in need. People come to make wishes at her **tomb**.

Marie Laveau's tomb

One man says he met a ghostly woman near the cemetery. She asked if he knew her. When he said no, she slapped him. Then she floated away.

He believes he met Marie Laveau. What do you believe?

SIGHTINGS OF MARIE LAVEAU

- Ghostly images appearing in photos taken near her tomb

- Woman dancing and chanting with followers on June 23

- Woman in white dress and tignon walking where Laveau used to live

THE VANISHING HITCHHIKER

Chicago is home to **Resurrection** Mary. In the 1930s, drivers began telling tales of a **hitchhiker**.

Chicago, Illinois

N
W E
S

NEED A RIDE?

Vanishing hitchhiker stories go back to at least the 1800s. In most, drivers pick up a woman who later disappears.

The stories described Mary, a young woman with blonde hair. She wore a white dress.

Some left with Mary from a dance club. Others picked her up along the road. She asked to be taken home along Archer Avenue. As they passed the Resurrection Cemetery gates, she would **vanish**!

LET ME OUT!

In 1976, a driver saw a girl locked inside the cemetery. Later, police found the gates bent and burned. The black marks looked like handprints.

SIGHTINGS OF RESURRECTION MARY

- Man dances with a girl all night and later watches her disappear at the cemetery gates on the way home (1930s)

- Many drivers tell of a woman trying to jump onto the side of their cars at night (1930s)

- People see a girl in a white dress dancing, but never entering or leaving the club (1970s)

- Drivers report hitting a young woman, who then disappears (1970s and 80s)

Legend says Mary went dancing before she died. She and her boyfriend had a fight.

Mary chose to walk home. But a car hit and killed her. She was buried in her white dress. Has she haunted Chicago ever since?

HISTORY CONNECTION

Anna Norkus could be the real Mary. She died after a night of dancing in 1927. She may have been buried in Resurrection Cemetery.

HAUNTED GRAVES OR JUST LEGENDS?

Long-ago sightings of Laveau's ghost may have been her daughter. Marie Laveau II also practiced voodoo. She looked a lot like her mother. But this cannot explain more recent sightings.

Late-night drivers are likely tired. Their sleepy minds could cause Resurrection Mary sightings. But could they have dreamt that they gave Mary a ride?

Would you go walking in a cemetery at night? If so, watch out for **restless** spirits!

GLOSSARY

hitchhiker—a person who travels by getting a free ride from a passing vehicle

legend—a story many people believe that has not been proven true

restless—unable to be still or at peace

resurrection—the act of rising to life from the dead

rituals—acts that are always performed in the same way, often as part of a religious ceremony

tignon—a scarf worn as a headdress in Louisiana

tomb—a chamber where a dead body is placed for burial

vanish—to disappear

voodoo—a religion practiced mainly in Haiti; Africans and Haitians brought a form of voodoo to Louisiana.

TO LEARN MORE

AT THE LIBRARY

Higgins, Nadia. *Ghosts*. Minneapolis, Minn.: Bellwether Media, 2014.

Person, Stephen. *Voodoo in New Orleans*. New York, N.Y.: Bearport Pub., 2011.

Schwartz, Alvin. *Scary Stories to Tell in the Dark*. New York, N.Y.: Harper, 2010.

ON THE WEB

Learning more about ghosts in cemeteries is as easy as 1, 2, 3.

1. Go to www.factsurfer.com.

2. Enter "ghosts in cemeteries" into the search box.

3. Click the "Surf" button and you will see a list of related web sites.

With factsurfer.com, finding more information is just a click away.

INDEX